Plains Indians of North America

'Before the coming of white men, we always had plenty; our children never cried from hunger, neither were our people in want.' These bitter words sum up the Indians' attitude towards the Europeans who settled in America and began grabbing their lands, plundering their villages and driving them farther and farther west. War between the two cultures inevitably broke out. The bloody clashes in the latter half of the last century culminated in the Indian massacre at Wounded Knee in 1890, where white man finally triumphed over Indian. Today, the majority of Indians still feel subordinated to the white man, despite years of struggling to redress the imbalance.

Robin May, an acknowledged authority on the American West, looks at the plight of the American Indians, tracing their history from the arrival of their ancestors some 30,000 years ago up to the modern day, as well as looking at the hopes they have for the future.

Original Peoples

PLAINS INDIANS
OF NORTH AMERICA

Robin May

Original Peoples

Frontispiece   *A hoop dancer from the Winnebago tribe displaying his expertise.*

First published in 1984 by
Wayland (Publishers) Limited
49 Lansdowne Place, Hove
East Sussex BN3 1HF, England

© Copyright 1984 Wayland (Publishers) Limited

ISBN 0 85078 421 2

Photoset by Planagraphic Typesetters Limited
Printed in Italy by G. Canale & C.S.p.A., Turin
Bound in the U.K. by The Garden City Press
Limited, Herts.

Contents

Introduction

A painting of Sitting Bull, Chief and Medicine Man of the Sioux tribe.

'Good shots, good riders, and the best fighters the sun ever shone on.' That was the opinion of a cavalry officer, named Frederick Benteen, about the warriors of the most famous of all the tribes on the American and Canadian Plains, the Sioux. Another officer stated that the Plains Indians were the best cavalry in the world!

Say 'Indian' in North America and elsewhere — or 'American Indian' or 'Red Indian' — and the chances are that people will think that you are talking about a Plains Indian. The Plains Indians are the most striking of all, with their proud faces, curved noses, high cheek bones, war bonnets — and their great leaders like Sitting Bull and Crazy Horse. Yet American and Canadian Indians as a whole are as different-looking as Europeans.

How then are the Plains Indians *the* Indians for most people? Why do names like Sioux, Cheyenne and Blackfoot thrill so many of us? The reasons will be given in this book, which is also about the sad story of Indians today. Many now prefer to be called Native Americans. After all, Columbus called them Indians because he thought he had reached the Indies — India — in 1492.

As we shall see, there were no horses on the Plains until white men brought them to the continent, so much of our story will be about the Plains Indians hunting, fighting and travelling on foot. The story mainly takes place on the 'Buffalo Plains', the High Plains that stretch from Texas into Canada. But it will extend to the foothills of the Rockies and to the wide Missouri river — and cover thousands of years.

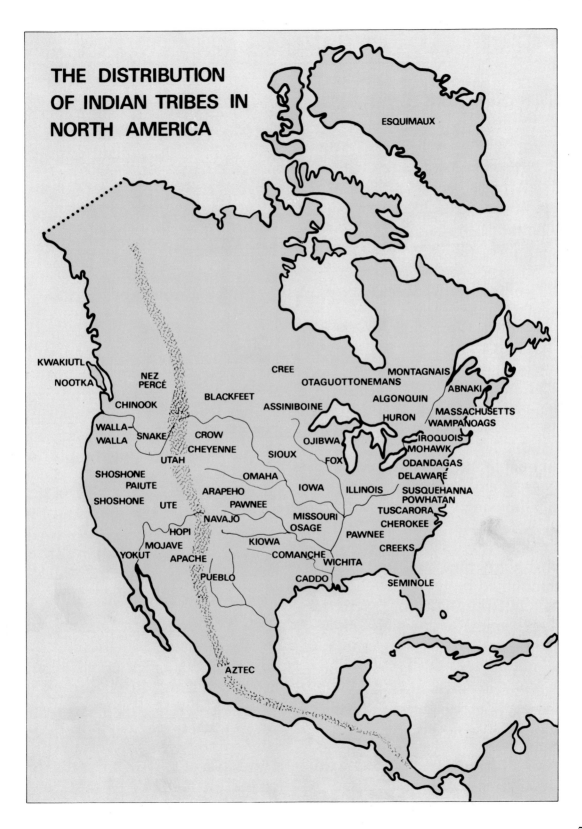

THE DISTRIBUTION
OF INDIAN TRIBES IN
NORTH AMERICA

ESQUIMAUX

KWAKIUTL

NOOTKA

CHINOOK

NEZ
PERCÉ

BLACKFEET

CREE

OTAGUOTTONEMANS

MONTAGNAIS

ALGONQUIN

ABNAKI

WALLA-
WALLA

SNAKE

CROW

CHEYENNE

UTAH

ASSINIBOINE

HURON

MASSACHUSETTS
WAMPANOAGS

SHOSHONE
PAIUTE

SHOSHONE

UTE

ARAPEHO

NAVAJO

HOPI

MOJAVE

YOKUT

APACHE

PUEBLO

OJIBWA

SIOUX

FOX

OMAHA

IOWA

PAWNEE

MISSOURI
OSAGE

KIOWA

COMANCHE

CADDO

WICHITA

IROQUOIS
MOHAWK

ODANDAGAS

DELAWARÉ

ILLINOIS

SUSQUEHANNA
POWHATAN

TUSCARORA

CHEROKEE

PAWNEE

CREEKS

SEMINOLE

AZTEC

7

Chapter 1 **The dog days**

Before the horse came

Between 20,000 and 30,000 years ago, waves of Asians crossed into North America across the narrow Bering Strait. From there they headed south, some even reaching the top of what is now South America. Even today the strait is less than 97 kilometres (60 miles) across, with islands in between. In prehistoric times the water was lower and sometimes there was no water at all, just dry land.

Most of the newcomers' descendants were to settle in Central and South America, some in what are now the United States and Canada. It is thought that not many settled on the vast Plains and those that did were sometimes driven off by droughts.

We know little of these Plains Indians until they got horses. All were mounted by the late eighteenth century. Before that, dogs were the transport animals, dragging belongings on 'travois' — sledges made from tent poles. Dogs could only drag short poles, so early Plains Indian tipis, or tepees (their buffalo-hide homes), were not tall.

On the eastern edge of the Plains, Indians farmed — along the Missouri river and elsewhere. On to the Plains came tribes driven

Members of the Nez Percé tribe with their dog travois.

westwards by other tribes who had acquired guns from French and British traders. The mighty Sioux were driven on to the Plains from the edge of the eastern forests by the Ojibways. Only the Santee Sioux stayed on the edge of the Plains in what is now Minnesota.

The Sioux's real name is Dakota (meaning allies). Sioux was a French word taken from another tribe's name for them, meaning enemy or serpents. The Cheyenne, too, came from the east. No one knows where the mighty Blackfoot came from.

They and many other tribes were on the Plains in the 'dog days'. Their days of the horse would be short, but thrilling, like those of other tribes.

Horse travois began to be used by tribes in the seventeenth century.

The hunters

For the Indians the buffalo was the most important of all their animal brothers, giving them food, shelter and clothing. They used almost every part of it. Buffalo hide was tanned and used to make such things as moccasins (the Indians' shoes) and leggings. Bones were made into arrowheads and knives; bridles were made of rawhide and hair; sinews made thread; even the stomach was used to make water buckets.

Hunting the buffalo on foot was a slow and often dangerous occupation. Some twenty or so families used to band together to encircle a small herd. Because the great beasts were not frightened of wolves, Indians sometimes used to wear wolf skins to get near a herd. The easiest way of killing the animals was to drive them over a cliff.

A herd of buffalo being driven over a cliff. The animal provided Indians with food, clothing and shelter.

Naturally, the coming of the horse transformed the slow-motion buffalo hunt into a wildly exciting affair. The Indians would risk injury or death as they sped in and out of the racing beasts.

Buffalo meat was nourishing and delicious, and until the 1870s there were millions of buffalo on the Plains. The destruction of the great herds by white hunters was partly to feed railroad workers and partly to

Two Indians hunting buffalo, dressed in wolf skins.

starve the Indians into submission. By 1889, there were just 541 buffalo left alive.

The Plains Indians also hunted moose (elk) and deer, but nothing equalled the buffalo hunt. Such hunts were well organized. A notable warrior would be chosen as hunt leader. Only war was more thrilling.

11

Foot soldiers of the Plains

For thousands of years Indians fought each other on foot. Wars cannot have been all that frequent on the endless Plains because enemies could have only been encountered occasionally. Battles must have been slow-motion affairs, with bows and arrows, clubs and spears. Not until the last half of the eighteenth century did all Plains Indians have horses. Then wars became frequent and certainly more exciting for the fighters.

The worst period for any Plains tribe, worse even than the final battles with the whites, must have been the exact moment when it was attacked by mounted enemies for the first time. The first time that Indian foot soldiers were attacked by rival Indians or whites with firearms must have been a grim moment as well. Yet it took some time to load those early guns and few Indians were then good shots. But the sight of men riding 3 metres (over 9 feet) high on strange and terrifying beasts must surely have stopped the heart of even the bravest warrior!

Before the coming of the horse, warfare was not a truly important part of a Plains Indian's life. It was hard enough to survive on the Plains without adding extra problems. Once the horse came, however, war would become a thrilling and regular event in the life of every Indian warrior on the Plains.

Below *Battles were more exciting once the Indians had horses.*

Right *A painting of a Comanche warrior, prepared for battle.*

13

Life in an Indian camp

Life on the Plains before the horse came remains rather mysterious, but we know enough of what happened later to understand something of it. For on the eastern edge of the Plains many tribes went on farming as they had done before. The women were usually the farmers.

Many of these farming Indians lived in earth lodges supported by log frames. The earth kept them warm in winter and cool in summer. The Wichita and other tribes on the southern Plains lived in thatched 'grass houses'. Maize, squash and beans were cultivated by the pre-horse Plains tribes. Every year there was a buffalo hunt, usually after a wild dance to lure the great beasts towards the village.

The women were responsible for

Indian women gathering wild rice.

A Sioux village, showing some women cleaning a buffalo skin.

putting every part of the buffalo to good use. Buffalo meat was plentiful once the horse had come, and tipis, as we have seen, got bigger. Many tribes also gave up farming for wandering on the Plains.

Indian children of both sexes were much loved, even spoiled, but were expected to take part in the life of the camp as they grew up. A Cheyenne boy would long to get into one of his tribe's warrior societies.

The Missouri villages became important trade centres early in the nineteenth century. Soon the old days of dog travois, and of Stone Age weapons, were just folk memories. Now there were guns and metal goods. There were many languages heard on the Plains and in the villages, but that presented no problem. Indian sign language was understood all over the Plains.

15

Strong medicine

Plains and other Indians had many beliefs in common. Living so close to Nature, the Earth for them was their mother, and they worshipped the Sun. On the Plains and elsewhere, Indians never owned land in the way white men owned it. You could not own your mother. True, when Indians were farmers, the land was important to them, and disputes over hunting rights could lead to war. Yet land was not sought after as much as whites hungered for it. For Indians, the land was a sacred trust.

As for 'medicine', which played such an important part in Indian life, it was an Indian's spirit protection — in life as well as in battle. It was a lucky charm taken very seriously.

Medicine men were part doctor, part priest. Long experience of extracting drugs from plants made many medicine men good doctors. American doctors now accept some 200 drugs used by Indians.

The medicine man was also a spiritual leader. The famous Sioux Sitting Bull was a war chief and a medicine man. Prophecy was expected of a medicine man, and Sitting Bull once provided sensational proof of his ability. In a trance he saw soldiers coming down like grasshoppers with heads down and hats off. They were falling into the Sioux camp upside down. His people rejoiced, for it was June 1876 and white soldiers were known to be

A young Cree performs the painful Sun Dance to prove himself a 'brave'.

near. The vision proved they would be defeated. Custer's Last Stand was only hours away!

Sitting Bull had taken part in the Sun Dance, a great ritual of the Plains Indians. Some braves stared at a pole and did a shuffling dance round it. Others, like Sitting Bull, had skewers through their chests attached to ropes fixed to a pole in the centre. They hung there until finally the skewers broke free. Many dancers were in a trance and felt nothing and some, like Sitting Bull, had visions. Strong medicine indeed!

A painting of White Cloud, Medicine Man of the Iowa Tribe.

Chapter 2 **The coming of the whites**

The arrival of the horse

The first white men in the American West were Spaniards. The date was 1540 and they were heading out of Mexico, looking for seven cities of gold — which turned out to be villages of mud and stone that shone in the sun. The expedition, led by Francisco de Coronado reached as far east as Kansas. More important from this book's point of view, horses escaped from the expedition, and others escaped later or were traded. It was in this way that the Plains Indians saw and, later, tamed the animal that revolutionized their lives.

A classic example of this is what happened to the Comanche. The artist George Catlin considered them 'the most unattractive and slovenly-looking race of Indians' on their feet, but on horseback he was surprised by the ease and grace of their movements. By this time they had become the dreaded 'Lords of the South Plains', wonderful riders who fought hard to stop the advance of Texan settlers.

The Comanches tried to stop the advance of settlers, like this family below.

The Spanish 'conquistadors' brought the horse to North America.

The Comanche, like the Sioux and other Plains Indians, regarded stealing horses as an even greater sport than war. Besides, horses were 'money' to Indians, useful for many purposes including for getting a wife. Even a difficult father might relent if the present of horses were good enough. We have seen how the buffalo hunt was transformed by the horse. So was the Indians' spirit life. A lone horseman on the mighty Plains of America and Canada with their endless horizons became a dreamer. He saw visions. He was nearer to his gods than he had ever been. For a century or so, longer in some areas, life seemed magical.

Warriors on horseback

For a short period, a magical one for the Plains Indians, warfare became a sport in which killing was only the fourth objective of the warrior! The period lasted about a century, ending when the wars in the West between Americans and Indians began in earnest in the 1860s.

The first object of the Plains Indian was to capture horses. The second was to count 'coup' on an enemy, which meant touching an enemy with a 'coup stick' and getting away safely. The third object was to rescue a fallen friend before his body could be disfigured by the enemy. Killing an enemy was less glorious than any of these. It was considered honourable to boast about one's feats, but the brave who lied was despised.

There were few white men in the West until large numbers started pouring across the Plains after gold was discovered in California in 1848. The few that were in the West were mainly 'Mountain Men' seeking beaver fur which was then fashionable for hats and coat trimmings. As these rugged trappers were almost white Indians, who fought with, lived with and often married Indian girls, they fitted into the landscape perfectly! It was too good to last — in the United States that is. Canada's Indians, as we shall see, were to be luckier, though even they were to lose true freedom.

Right *Braves returning to their camp with some stolen horses.*

Below *Typical weapons, tools and clothing of a Plains Indian.*

Little Big Horn

Long before the American Civil War broke out in 1861, the South Plains had erupted into warfare between Americans and Indians. Comanche and Kiowa warriors, in particular, used terror tactics to try and drive white intruders out of their territory.

Yet there was no real trouble further north, until war broke out in 1854 because a settler accused a Sioux of killing one of his cows! Not until 1890 would the Plains' Wars end.

Counting coup and other Indian tactics were little use against the newcomers. Also, because Indians valued their freedom so much, Indian leaders, except the very greatest, never had total control over their independent warriors. A junior American officer could expect to be obeyed automatically. An Indian chief could not. The Indians were too democratic when fighting an enemy for whom war was not merely a great game. And when the continent was spanned by rail in 1869, it became easy to rush soldiers to the West.

Yet the Plains Indians fought valiantly and, finally, desperately. Chief Red Cloud of the Sioux won a resounding victory over the whites in the 1860s, saving the Powder river country for his people for a time. Gradually, though, sheer numbers and new rapid-firing rifles put the Indians on the defensive. Worse, literally millions of buffalo were slaughtered, leading to starvation for many Indians. And the new railroads carried many thousands of settlers West.

The Plains Indians' greatest victory came in 1876 at the Battle of Little Big Horn in Montana — Custer's Last Stand. Sioux, Cheyenne and Arapaho overwhelmed the Seventh Cavalry, killing all Custer's immediate command of about 215 men and many more of the regiment. This was really the last great stand of the Indians, too.

Chief Red Cloud of the Sioux.

Right *Custer's 'Last Stand': the Battle of Little Big Horn in 1876.*

Wounded Knee 1890

News of Custer's defeat enraged Americans who were busy celebrating a century of independence from Britain. The troops pouring West could fight in the winter, unlike the Indians. It was all they could do to survive now that the buffalo had been almost exterminated. The last warriors were rounded up, though Sitting Bull and several thousand Sioux, as we shall see, sought refuge in Canada. Meanwhile, the greatest Sioux warrior, Crazy Horse, was forced to surrender. He was soon to be murdered 'resisting arrest'. At Little Big Horn he had shouted to his warriors: 'Today is a good day to fight! Today is a good day to die!'

Now was a time for other Indians to make 'last stands'. The northern Cheyenne were banished to rot in Indian territory on a barren reservation. Many died. So some 280 men,

The Battle of Wounded Knee in 1890, where a band of Sioux were killed.

24

女Big Foot
Copyrighted by the
Northwestern Photo Co.   Chadron Neb

women and children set out for their Montana home, pursued by troops. Some got back safely; others were caught and locked up in a hut at Fort Robinson, Nebraska, threatened with a return to their living hell.

One night they broke out. The women had hidden the parts of the men's rifles beneath their clothes when they were rounded up. Men grabbed more guns from soldiers shot as they erupted from the fort. It took days to kill, wound or capture

Chief Big Foot of the Sioux lies dead in the snow after the battle.

the fugitives. So heroic had they been that public opinion forced the authorities to send the survivors home.

The Plains Wars finally ended at Wounded Knee in 1890, when Custer's old regiment, the Seventh Cavalry, wiped out a band of Sioux. Peace — a bitter one — had come to the Plains.

Peace on the Northern Plains

Though Canada had no Wild West to compare with America's, the situation on the Canadian Plains became very dangerous in the early 1870s. The great Blackfoot nation — that part of it which lived in Canada — was under threat. The buffalo was vanishing fast and the Indians were being ravaged by white diseases, especially smallpox. Vicious American traders were selling the Indians rot-gut whisky, and in 1873 a gang massacred peaceful Assiniboine for alleged horse-stealing. Others killed an entire camp of Piegan Blackfoot.

The Canadian government, now recognizing its duty to the Indians and law-abiding whites, raised the famous 'Mounties'. A scarlet-coated force of some 275 North-West Mounted Police headed westwards wearing a colour that the Indians could trust. The red-coated British soldier had earned their respect down the years. Forts were built, the whisky traders rapidly headed south, and a treaty was made with Crowfoot, Chief of the Blackfoot confederacy of tribes.

So successful was this handful of police in inspiring trust that there was little trouble when some 4,000 Sioux, including the great Sitting Bull, sought shelter in Canada from troops eager to avenge Custer. Superintendent James Walsh toured Sioux camps sometimes with as few as six men, and explained Canada's laws to warriors with white scalps on their belts.

The Sioux wished to stay, but there was now not enough food to feed Canada's Indians, some of whom were enemies of the Sioux. By 1881, nearly all had been persuaded to go south, including Sitting Bull.

In 1885, a rebellion of French Canadian half-breeds, called Métis, and Cree Indians erupted on the Plains. It was led by a Métis named Louis Riel. Fortunately for Canada, the Blackfoot remained at peace. A handful of Mounties representing Queen Victoria had saved Canada from a major Indian war. Honesty and fair play had paid off.

Louis Riel, who led a rebellion in Canada in 1885.

26

Modern-day Mounties in the scarlet uniform they wear for formal occasions.

The Canadian way

After the Riel Rebellion, Canada's Plains Indians faced many of the same problems as Indians did south of the border. Even those who had not joined in the rebellion could not help lamenting that the old, free days had gone.

True, the Canadian government treated its 'charges' more honourably than did the Americans, and there were fewer changes of policy. Yet the loss of the old freedom was a bitter one. Records show that the two major problems the Mounties faced were horse-stealing and drink. The former, so recently an exciting sport, was now illegal. As for drink, too many people were eager to sell it to the Indians whom it harmed so much.

Treaties were made covering huge areas of land. These were ceded to the Crown which, through the government, took on certain obligations. Indians were given reserves (as Canadians call reservations), annual cash payments, hunting and fishing rights, and education services.

Old ways died hard, however. A young Cree, called Almighty Voice, escaped from a Mountie post in Saskatchewan after a foolish guard told him he would be hanged for stealing a government steer. When he killed a sergeant sent to bring him in, a two-year man hunt began. It ended in a thicket in 1897, where Almighty Voice was cornered with two boys,

The death of Almighty Voice.

one of them his cousin. Three whites and one of the boys died on the first day of the battle. The next day artillery was brought up and went into action the following dawn.

The next morning saw the end of the battle. Volunteers found Almighty Voice dead and his cousin dying. On a tree was scrawled in Cree: 'Here died three braves', referring to the three white men who had died. 'He was a great warrior,' said a Mountie officer later, 'the last of his valiant breed.'

An Indian camp on the shores of Lake Huron. The tipis and canoes are made of the bark of trees.

Chapter 3 **The bitterest years**

The road from Wounded Knee

In 1887, three years before the final tragedy of the Indian Wars at Wounded Knee, an act was passed by the US Government. It was called the Dawes Act after its champion, Henry Dawes. It set a pattern for a number of unfortunate and sometimes disastrous measures whose effects are felt to this day.

Well-meaning whites and land grabbers both thought that individual Indians should own land. Yet the only real power that an Indian who wished to remain an Indian had was being a member of his tribe. The Dawes Act gave millions of Indian acres to whites. For instance, instead of one great reservation, the Sioux now had six small ones, leaving 9 million acres for whites to grab.

In their misery, the Sioux turned to a new religion, called the Ghost Dance, that was sweeping the West: a peaceful one that proclaimed the disappearance of the whites and the return of the buffalo. But the Sioux thought it a warlike creed and that white bullets could not harm them. This, plus bad luck and bad management, led to the destruction of Chief Big Foot's band at Wounded Knee.

Meanwhile, the Dawes Act was putting pressure on all Indians. As we shall see, they were soon forbidden to be 'real' Indians.

Every Indian family was meant to have 160 acres. But few could cope with the 'land sharks' who 'advised' them on property, even Indians who understood English quite well. The result was that between 1887 and 1934 Indians lost 86 million out of their 138 million acres.

On the left is Wovoka, a Paiute Indian, who founded and led the Ghost Dance religious movement.

GRAND RUSH

FOR THE

INDIAN

TERRITORY !

NOW IS THE CHANCE

TO

PROCURE A HOME

In this Beautiful Country!

Over 15,000,000 Acres of Land

NOW OPEN FOR SETTLEMENT !

Being part of the Land bought by the Government in 1866 from the Indians for the Freedmen.

THE FINEST TIMBER !
THE RICHEST LAND !
THE FINEST WATERED !
WEST OF THE MISSISSIPPI RIVER.

Every person over 21 years of age is entitled to 160 acres, either by pre-emption or homestead, who wishes to settle in the Indian Territory. It is estimated that over Fifty Thousand will move to this Territory in the next ninety days. The Indians are rejoicing to have the whites settle up this country.

The Grand Expedition will Leave Independence May 7, 1879

Independence is situated at the terminus of the Kansas City, Lawrence & Southern Railroad. The citizens of Independence have laid out and made a splendid road to these lands; and they are prepared to furnish emigrants with complete outfits, such as wagons, agricultural implements, dry goods, groceries, lumber and stock. They have also opened an office there for general information to those wishing to go to the Territory, IT COSTS NOTHING TO BECOME A MEMBER OF THIS COLONY.

Persons passing through Kansas City will apply at the office of K. C. L. & S R R. opposite Union Depot, for Tickets.

ABOUT THE LANDS.

In answer to inquiries concerning these government lands in the Indian Territory, Col. E. C. Boudinot sends the following from Washington:

FIRST—In reply I will say that the United States, by treaties made in 1866, purchased from Indian tribes, in the Indian Territory, about 14,000,000 acres of land.

SECOND—These lands were bought from the Creeks, Seminoles, Choctaws and Chickasaws, by their treaty of 1866.

The Creeks, by their treaty of 1866, sold to the United States 3,250,560 acres, for the sum of $975,168. The Seminoles, by their treaty of 1866, sold to the United States 2,169,080 acres, for the sum of $325,362.

The Choctaws and Chickasaws, by their treaty of 1866, sold to the United States the "leased lands" lying west of 98 degrees of west longitude, for the sum of $300,000. The number of acres in this tract is not specified in the treaty, but it contains about 7,000,000 acres. (See 14th vol. Statutes at Large, pages 756, 769 and 786.)

Of these ceded lands the United States has since appropriated for the use of the Sac and Foxes 479,667 acres and for the Pottawatomies 575,877 acres, making a total of 1,055,542 acres. These Indians occupy these lands by virtue of treaties and acts of Congress. By an unratified agreement, the Wichita Indians are now occupying 743,610 acres of these ceded lands. I presume some action will be taken by the United States government to permanently locate the Wichitas upon the lands they now occupy. The title, however, to these lands is still in the United States.

By executive order, Kiowa, Comanche, Arrapahoe, and other wild Indians, have been brought upon a portion of the ceded lands, but such lands are a part of the public domain of the United States, and have all been surveyed and sectionised.

A portion of these 14,000,000 acres of land, however, has not been appropriated by the United States for the use of other Indians and all probability never will be.

THIRD—These unappropriated lands are situated immediately west of the 97th degree of west longitude and south of the Cherokee territory. The soil is well adapted for the production of corn, wheat and other cereals. It is unsurpassed for grazing, and is well watered and timbered.

FOURTH—The United States have an absolute and unembarrassed title to every acre of these 14,000,000 acres, unless it be to the 1,054,544 now occupied by the Sac and Fox and Pottawatomie Indians. The Indian title has been extinguished. The articles of the treaties with the Creeks and Seminoles, by which they sold their lands, begin with the statement that the lands are ceded "in compliance with the desire of the United States to locate other Indians and freedmen thereon." By the express terms of these treaties the lands bought by the United States were not intended for the exclusive use of other Indians" as has been so often asserted. They were bought as much for the negroes of the country as for Indians.

ADDRESS

WM. C. BRANHAM,

Independence, Kansas.

To parties accompanying my Colony, I would advise them to purchase their Outfit at Independence, Kas., I have examined Stock and Prices of Goods, such as Wagons, Plows, Lumber, Dry Goods, Groceries, and, in fact, everything that is needed by Parties settling upon new Land, and find them as cheap as they can be bought in the East.

RESPECTFULLY YOURS,

Col. C. C. CARPENTER.

P. S.—Parties will have no trouble in getting transportation at Independence for hauling their goods into the Territory.   C. C. C.

Advertisements, like this one, encouraged white settlers to buy land in Indian Territory in 1879.

Proof that the Dawes Act was partly a fraud is the fact that Indians of the south-western deserts mainly kept their lands — because the whites did not want them! Some whites killed to get land — to judge by the crime statistics in some areas. It was quicker than being an 'adviser'.

Killing a culture

The Dawes Act led to other 'improvements' for Indians. Indian religions, being considered heathen ones, were attacked. Indian adults and children alike were exposed to Christianity whether they wanted it or not. It hardly helped that rival preachers descended on reservations. Most Indians were as religious as the most religious white men, but their beliefs were — until modern times — rejected. Meanwhile, Indian men were forced to have their hair cut short. In such ways were the cultures of the Indians almost destroyed, almost but not quite.

Naturally, some Indians became property-loving householders like the whites, and some did very well — and still do — from oil finds on their reservations. Far more had their gains snatched away from them.

Some Indians escaped from misery to join Wild West shows that toured East and West alike. Buffalo Bill's Wild West Show was the best and most famous. William Cody, who ran it, was a genuine Westerner whose nickname came from the number of buffalo he had slaughtered to feed railroad builders. Yet he genuinely liked Indians and they liked him, though he had fought them. He brought his show to Europe on several occasions, the most famous being his visit to Britain in 1887, Queen Victoria's Golden Jubilee year.

Some said — and still say — that it was insulting for Indians to take part in mock battles. Why? It was better than life on a reservation, besides which Cody respected them. He and they were part of the Old West, which had already gone forever.

Buffalo Bill's Wild West Show in London in 1887.

A poster advertising Buffalo Bill's show.

Chapter 4 The Plains Indian today

A new deal?

In the First World War, a number of Indians served in the American Army. This had one excellent result. These volunteers got the vote, and in 1924 all Indians were officially given it. In fact, New Mexico and Arizona held back the vote from illiterate and off-reservation Indians until 1959.

Not until 1930, did the death-rate among Indians at last start to decline. Up till then the phrase, 'The Vanishing American', was all too true. Yet conditions were still grim on most reservations. Few Indians wanted to be farmers and those who did were often held back by the wretchedness of the soil on their

A Crow reservation in Montana at the turn of the century.

Indians and white men alike were easy prey to unscrupulous rot-gut whisky distillers.

tribal reservations.

When Franklin D. Roosevelt became president in 1932, the nation was in a period called the Depression. Business, which had boomed in the 1920s, had slumped. Fortunately, Roosevelt included Indians in his plans to revitalize the country. The Dawes Act was reversed, which saved the tribal system. 'Community ownership and control' was the new watchword, and more Indians were brought in to work in the Indian Service.

It was not as easy as that. Too many reservations on the Plains and elsewhere are on poor land. Yet if Indians leave the reservation, their home, and head for cities, too many fail to succeed because of lack of qualifications. Indians are still a prey to disease and alcohol, and their life expectancy is far lower than that of whites.

Red Power

The 1960s and '70s saw a number of Indians fighting publicly for their rights with words and sometimes with deeds. Plains Indians were among the leaders. The 1950s had seen one particularly disastrous policy put into operation. Several reservations were actually closed, allegedly with the best of intentions. The timber-rich Menominee of Wisconsin was one of those closed and a proud and successful people disintegrated as a tribe. Not until 1973 was this termination policy reversed. Many believe that it was the timber that appealed to white termination promoters, not goodwill . . .

Against such a background and years of grievance, militant Indians started preaching Red Power in the 1960s (following the example of

An amicable end to the siege of Wounded Knee in 1973.

Black Power). The American Indian Movement, which includes Canada's Indians, demanded Indian rights. The militants lost much public sympathy, however, in 1973 when Wounded Knee was once again the scene of action. Much of it was in fact due to hostility between traditional Indians, notably the local Sioux, and militants or 'progressive' Indians. There was violence and a number of killings, while the militants who invaded the Bureau of Indian Affairs in Washington also destroyed property. With far fewer Native Americans than there are

The American Indian Movement siezed the village of Wounded Knee to draw attention to its grievances.

Blacks, support is much needed.

The good side of the militancy has been a new pride among Indians. They often suffer humiliation off the reservations from local whites. The new pride among many is backed up by Indian newspapers written for and read by — Indians.

Meanwhile, with the help of lawyers, many tribes are getting financial compensation for land losses in the past.

37

Hope for the young?

Indians are firm believers in family life. About half the United States' Indians live on reservations and more than half of Canada's Indians. The governments of both countries are responsible for educating young Indians and those children who attend reservation schools are at least on 'home ground'.

Indian children in mainly white schools may take time to adjust, not least to teasing. If it rains, the Indian child may be teased about rain dances. Nicknames like Sitting Bull and Geronimo may lower a child's morale, along with Indians continually war-whooping and 'biting the dust' on TV. Some children drop out. Others are taken away by welfare authorities from their homes for a 'better' life in boarding schools, or with white foster parents. The suicide rate on some reservations is high amongst the young.

Yet more and more young Indians on both sides of the border are becoming farmers, doctors, lawyers, and mechanics. Some hold high positions in government, and excel in the arts. Yet the chances of reservation-born Indians getting on are still not very high. Only one area, Oklahoma, once Indian Territory, has so many people of Indian descent that politicians often claim a little Indian blood when running for office, even if they have not a drop!

Fortunately for the Indian child, he or she usually lives in a society that respects the old, believes in the family, and tries to live in harmony with nature. The young Indian, on the Plains and elsewhere, does not have to be a competitor in life if he does not want to be one. Many North American whites have come to see that Indian life at its best, for young and old, is to be envied.

Bullhead hamlet on the Sioux reservation in North Dakota.

A young Crow Indian, dressed for a tribal gathering in Montana.

Reservations

Many Plains and other Indians decide to live off their reservations. A scheme to help them was started in 1952, which is now known as the Employment Assistance Program. It has helped to train Indians and to find them jobs, also to house them. The big cities attract some; sadly, many find themselves doing un-skilled jobs and living in poor accommodation. On the reservation the Indian is part of a whole; but this is not the case in some run-down areas of a big city.

There are some 285 American reservations, the biggest on the Plains being the Sioux reservations in South Dakota. One of the most beautiful is the Shoshoni reservation in Wyoming. The tribe supported the United States against its tribal enemies and, unlike many tribes, kept much of its homeland.

There are Indian gatherings all over the Plains, which tourists may enjoy, but which are primarily for the Indians themselves. Some Indians shine on the sports fields, others take part in rodeos. Plains Indians normally dress as white Americans do, but they will dress up in all their finery for the right occasions.

As for living the old life, perhaps only on the northern Plains of Canada, its mountains in the West and the lakes and forests to the East, can something like that be lived.

What is certain is that Indian culture and heritage, once despised by whites, can now be an important part of an Indian's life again. On the Plains and elsewhere, Indian hearts beat with pride.

Left *Jim Thorpe, the Red Indian Olympic champion.*

An all-Indian rodeo in Oregon state.

Canadian Indians today

What are the practical advantages of being an Indian? A look at the 'status' Indians of Canada — some 290,000 of them — can give us a clue. These are registered under the Indian Act and are the responsibility of the Indian and Inuit Affairs Program, which was started by the Department of Indian and Northern Development. There is a minister in charge of the department.

Apart from the obvious fact that an Indian can live on his reserve, he can possess land on it, his property cannot be seized, and he cannot be taxed on his income earned on the reserve. He has hunting, fishing and trapping rights and if, at the age of 21, he wishes to leave the reserve and give up his Indian status, he is entitled to certain funds held by his band of Indians. Some Canadian

Indian dancers at a tribal gathering in Alberta, Canada.

These Canadian Chippewa Indians run a market-gardening business.

Indians have oil on their reserves, so the young man may leave with a considerable sum of money.

Indians are always on the look-out for ideas from white people which may have hidden traps. In November 1983, Plains Indian leaders of Canada and the Assembly of First Nations welcomed a report by the government suggesting self-government. Yet an Indian expert on her people's politics, Marie Smallface Marule, suggested caution. Back in 1969 a rather similar plan turned out to be nothing more than an elimination of Indian land rights. This new plan is much better, but is being studied very carefully. Says Ms Marule: 'Let us as Indians make haste slowly!'

Chapter 5 **Into the future**

What does the future hold for America's Indians? If Secretary of the Interior James Watt (a member of President Reagan's Administration until his outspokenness led to his resignation in 1983) had his way, there would be no reservations. He called for their abolition, said that the Indian way of life was a failure, and that the reservation system had not worked!

True, the system is not ideal, but it has helped save the Indian way of life. As for the suggestion that the Indian way of life was a failure, Mary Hanson of Whittier, California, pointed out that if 'our ancestors had followed the environmental ethics of the American Indians . . . America would still be known as "the beautiful".'

The Red Indian of romance . . .

. . . and modern-day reality?

Watt, of course, went 'over the top', but the problem is not that simple. There is enormous mineral wealth still to be tapped in the American West, including oil and coal. Some of this wealth must be used. Yet if Indian land is exploited, it must be to the benefit first and foremost of the Indians. There were too few of them — perhaps a million when the whites arrived in America — to hold their lands. But hold what they now have they must — not only for their sakes but for Americans in general. The same applies to Canada's Indians.

The Plains Indian on horseback — in Wyoming, on the Plains of Texas, in Alberta. The whole world knows that picture. That is the Indian of romance. But the Indian who worshipped the Earth as his Mother? Surely the Indian is entitled to lead his own life in peace on a portion of the earth he once worshipped?

Glossary

Buffalo In fact, the American buffalo is a bison. It roamed in great herds over the Plains and Prairies until white settlers almost made it extinct.

Coup It was considered more courageous in a battle to touch an enemy warrior with your 'coup stick' and escape, rather than to kill him.

Custer, General George (1839-76) He was not the Indian-hater of legend, but he was very ambitious. His 'Last Stand' against the Sioux, Cheyenne and Arapaho in 1876 earned him a place in Wild West history.

Ghost Dance A religious movement which began in the 1880s. It said that the white man would be driven from the Plains and that the buffalo would return. Believers danced a special dance.

Indian Territory From the early years of the 19th century, most Indians were forced westwards by land-hungry whites. A vast area, known as Indian Territory, was created, but much of it was later wanted by the whites. What was left of it became the State of Oklahoma in 1907. The descendants of many tribes from all over the USA live there today — proudly.

Medicine The magical powers that a person had, which gave strength in war or in hunting.

Medicine man A spiritual leader who was part priest, part doctor, part prophet. Medicine men might also be warriors.

Mountain men Trappers, who got their name from the Rocky Mountains. They roamed the Plains too.

Plains Most of this book is set on the 'High Plains' that stretch from Alberta to Saskatchewan in Canada to Texas. However, the story of the Plains Indians stretches westwards into the foothills of the Rockies and eastwards on to the Prairies.

Red Indian Indians are shades of brown. A possible explanation of 'Red' Indian or Redskin is that some of the first white men in the East saw light-skinned Indians. When they became tanned, they looked reddish, then copper-coloured.

Sun dance An important religious ceremony, held once a year when a tribe gathered for the summer buffalo hunt. Young men would often torture themselves. The wounds that resulted from this were considered a mark of distinction and a source of pride.

Tipi Sometimes spelt tepee or teepee. The conical tent used by Plains Indians. They were made from 11 to 22 buffalo skins. These were used to cover the wooden poles that were arranged in a circle and brought together at the top to form a cone shape. A hole was left in the top to allow the smoke from the fire to escape. The inside walls were often lined with skins for warmth. The entrance to a tipi always faced east, towards the sunrise.

Travois A frame built with two poles, which was dragged behind a dog and then, from the late 1600s, behind a horse. It carried an Indian family's belongings.

War bonnet Feathered headdress.

Books to read

Brandon, William, (editor), *Indians* (American Heritage Publishing Co.)

Brown, Dee, *Bury my Heart at Wounded Knee: an Indian History of the American West* (Fontana)

Capps, Benjamin, *The Great Chiefs* (Time-Life Books)

Gibson, Michael, *The American Indian* (Wayland)

Hagan, William T., *American Indians* (University of Chicago Press)

Luling, Virginia, *Indians of the North American Plains* (Macdonald)

May, Robin, *The Wild West* (Macdonald)

Palmer, Ann, *Growing up with the Red Indians* (Wayland)

Tanner, Ogden, *The Canadians* (Time-Life Books)

Taylor, Colin, *Warriors of the Plains* (Hamlyn)

Turner, Geoffrey, *Indians of North America* (Blandford)

Utley, Robert, *The Last Days of the Sioux Nation* (Yale University Press)

White, John M., *Everyday Life of the North American Indian* (Batsford)

Wilson, Maurice, & Thompson, George, *A Closer Look at Plains Indians* (Hamish Hamilton)

The American books listed above are available through bookshops, some being in public libraries. For those wanting detailed information about Plains tribes, the University of Oklahoma Press has published books about them — and other Indians.

Acknowledgements

The illustrations in this book came from the following sources: Alberta Government 42; BBC Hulton Picture Library 16, 32; *frontispiece* (M. Timothy O'Keefe), 10 (Jeff Foott), 41 (Joseph Van Wormer) — all from Bruce Coleman Ltd; Mary Evans Picture Library 11; The Mansell Collection 26, 44; Robin May/U.S. Signal Corps 22, 25; Peter Newark's WESTERN AMERICANA 6, 8, 9, 13, 14, 15, 17, 19, 20, 21, 23, 24, 28, 29, 31, 33, 34, 35; Oklahoma State Senate 40; Popperfoto 36, 37, 45; Colin Taylor 38, 39; U.S. National Anthropological Archives, Smithsonian Institution 30; Wayland Picture Library 7, 12, 18, 27, 43; ZEFA *cover*.

Index